Scott Foresman

Scott Foresman Reading
Let's Learn Together

Good Times We Share

Take a Closer Look

Let's Learn Together

Favorite Things Old and New

Take Me There

Surprise Me!

PEARSON

Scott Foresman

About the Cover Artist

Maryjane Begin and her family live in Providence, Rhode Island, where she teaches college students when she is not working on her own art. Many of her illustrations—even imaginary places—show how things in Providence look.

Cover illustration © Maryjane Begin

ISBN 0-328-03929-2

4 5 6 7 8 9 10 V063 10 09 08 07 06 05 04 03

Scott Foresman Reading
Let's Learn Together

Program Authors

Peter Afflerbach

James Beers

Camille Blachowicz

Candy Dawson Boyd

Wendy Cheyney

Deborah Diffily

Dolores Gaunty-Porter

Connie Juel

Donald Leu

Jeanne Paratore

Sam Sebesta

Karen Kring Wixson

PEARSON

Scott Foresman

Editorial Offices: Glenview, Illinois • Parsippany, New Jersey • New York, New York
Sales Offices: Parsippany, New Jersey • Duluth, Georgia • Glenview, Illinois
Coppell, Texas • Ontario, California • Mesa, Arizona

Contents

Let's Learn Together

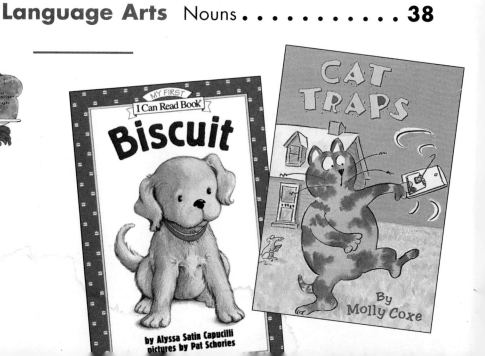

4

Unit 3

5

Let's Learn Together

What can
we learn when
we all work
together?

The Big Mess

by B. G. Hennessy   illustrated by Christine Davenier

"Who made this mess?"
said Tess.

"Can you help guess?"
said Ben.

A mess in the hall.
A mess on the wall.

A mess on the floor.
A mess on the door.

So, was it the dog?
Was it the cat?

No, guess again.
It was baby Matt!

Now you see who made the mess.

But who cleaned it up?
Can you guess?

The Little Red Hen

by Patricia and Fredrick McKissack

illustrated by John Sandford

"Who will help me?" said
the Little Red Hen.

"Who me?"

"Why me?"

"Oh, no. Not me."

20

So the Little Red Hen
did it by herself.

"Who will help me?" said
the Little Red Hen.

So the Little Red Hen
did it by herself.

"Who will help me now?"

"No. I cannot."

"No. No. I cannot."

"No. No. No. I cannot."

So the Little Red Hen
did it by herself.

"Who will help me?" said
the Little Red Hen.

"Not now."

"No. No. Not now."

"Not now. Not now."

So the Little Red Hen
did it by herself.

"Who will help me?" said
the Little Red Hen.

"I will, next time."

"Yes. Next time."

"Yes. Yes. Next time."

So the Little Red Hen
did it by herself.

"Who will help me now?"
said the Little Red Hen.

"I cannot help."

"I cannot help."

"I cannot help."

So the Little Red Hen
did it by herself.

"Who will help me?" said
the Little Red Hen.

"I will!"

"Yes. I will too."

"I want to help too."

33

But the Little Red Hen said,
"No. No. No. You did not help me.
I will eat by myself."

About the Authors

Patricia and Fredrick McKissack met when they were teenagers. They both loved books. After they got married, they wrote books together.

The McKissacks like growing things in a garden just as the Little Red Hen does.

Reader Response

Let's Talk

The Little Red Hen does not get any help. What would you do if this happened to you?

Let's Think

Little Red Hen does not share her bread. Is she fair? Why or why not?

Test Prep
Let's Write

Name the animals who did not help Little Red Hen. Write a job each one can do next time.

Let's Act

Choose an animal from the story.

Make a mask for that animal.

1. Get what you need.
2. Make a face.
3. Add yarn ties.
4. Act out the story.

Use your own words.

Language Arts

Nouns

A noun is a word that names a person, place, animal, or thing.

The **boy** is by the **barn**.

The **pigs** eat **corn**.

What do the nouns in each sentence name?

Person	**Place**	**Animal**	**Thing**
boy	barn	pigs	corn

Talk

Talk about the picture.
Use nouns.
Tell where each noun belongs on the chart.

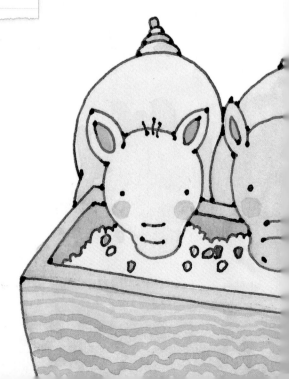

Write

Write the sentences. Circle the nouns.

1. The farmer drives the tractor.

2. The girl picks beans.

3. The farm is big.

Write your own sentences.

Use nouns.

Circle the nouns.

Yes, We Want Some Too!

by Susan McCloskey

illustrated by Rosario Valderrama

The ten gray gulls are hungry.

They want some clams.

Mmm, good!

Yes, we want some too, please.

The black crows are hungry.

They want some fish.

Mmm, good!

Yes, we want some too, please.

The red hens are hungry.

They want some corn.

Mmm, good!

Yes, we want some too, please.

The green frogs are hungry.

They want some flies.

Ick! No flies for us!

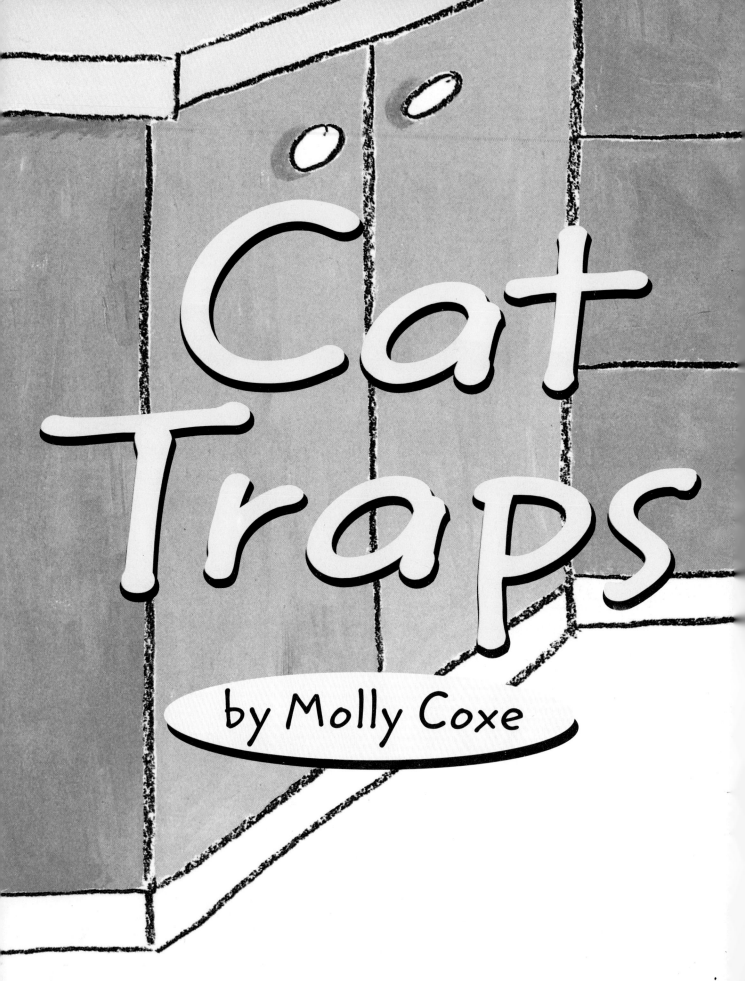

Cat Traps

by Molly Coxe

Cat wants a snack.

Cat sets a trap.

Cat gets a bug.

Ugh!

Cat wants a snack.
Cat sets a trap.

Cat gets a pig.

Too big!

Cat wants a snack.

Cat sets a trap.

Cat gets a fish.
Swish!

Cat wants
a snack.
Cat sets
a trap.

Cat gets
a frog?

No, a dog!

Cat wants a snack.
Cat sets a trap.
Cat gets a duck.

Bad luck!

Cat wants a snack.

Cat sets a trap.

Cat gets—
a cat!

Drat.

Cat wants a snack.
Cat sets a trap.

Cat gets some chow.

Meow!

About the Author

Molly Coxe uses part of her garage as her studio. She works there while her children are in school. Her family has two cats, a dog, and a rabbit. One of their cats looks like the cat in *Cat Traps*.

Reader Response

Let's Talk

Pretend you are an animal that Cat trapped. What would you say to Cat?

Let's Think

Cat sets a trap for the girl. How does he get a snack from her?

 Test Prep

Let's Write

Pretend you are Cat. Write in your Cat journal. Tell about your day. Tell what happened first, next, and last.

Make a Snack Mobile

Cats like snacks.
Boys and girls like snacks too.
Work with your classmates.
Make a snack mobile.

1. Draw a picture of
   your favorite snack.

2. Cut out your picture.

3. Punch a hole at the top.

4. Put a piece of string
   through the hole.

5. Tie your picture to a hanger.
   Your teacher may hang your
   mobile.

Language Arts

Nouns for One and More than One

Sometimes **–s** is added to the end of a noun. An **–s** tells about more than one.

Mary has one **dog**.

Tom has two **dogs** .

Which word tells about more than one?

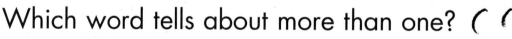

One	More than One
dog	dogs

76

Talk

Name the nouns in the picture. Where does each noun go on the chart?

Write

Write the sentences.
Draw one line under the nouns that tell about one.
Draw two lines under the nouns that tell about more than one.

1. The snake is green.
2. The bird eats seeds.
3. The frogs can jump.

Write your own sentences. Use nouns that tell about one and nouns that tell about more than one.

My Buddy, Stan

by Deborah Eaton

illustrated by Shelly Hehenberger

I am Pug.

This is my buddy, Stan.

Stan is lots of fun.

I let Stan pat me.
I let him brush me.
He likes it!

I let Stan run with me.

I let him jump with me.

He likes it!

I let Stan play with me.
I let him tug at a stick.
He likes it!

I let Stan feed me too.
That snack smells good.
Yum! More, please.

Time to go to sleep.

But Stan wants to hug me.

I can tell.

I like it!
So I let him.
What a good hug!

Good boy, Stan.
Good boy!

Biscuit

by Alyssa Satin Capucilli

illustrated by Pat Schories

This is Biscuit.

Biscuit is small.

Biscuit is yellow.

Time for bed, Biscuit!

Woof, woof!
Biscuit wants to play.

Time for bed, Biscuit!

Woof, woof!

Biscuit wants a snack.

Time for bed, Biscuit!

Woof, woof!

Biscuit wants a drink.

Time for bed, Biscuit!

Woof, woof!

Biscuit wants to hear a story.

Time for bed, Biscuit!

Woof, woof!

Biscuit wants his blanket.

Time for bed, Biscuit!

Woof, woof!

Biscuit wants his doll.

Time for bed, Biscuit!

Woof, woof!

Biscuit wants a hug.

Time for bed, Biscuit!

Woof, woof!

Biscuit wants a kiss.

Time for bed, Biscuit!

Woof, woof!

Biscuit wants a light on.

Woof!

Biscuit wants to be tucked in.

Woof!

Biscuit wants one more kiss.

Woof!

Biscuit wants one more hug.

Woof!

Biscuit wants to curl up.

Sleepy puppy.
Good night, Biscuit.

About the Author and the Illustrator

Author

Alyssa Satin Capucilli lives with her husband and two children. She has written other books about Biscuit. One is called *Biscuit Finds a Friend.*

Pat Schories has a dog named Spike. She used Spike as the model for Biscuit. Ms. Schories has illustrated other books for children.

Illustrator

Puppy

by Lee Bennett Hopkins

We bought our puppy
   A brand new bed
But he likes sleeping
   On mine instead.

I'm glad he does
   'Cause I'd miss his cold nose

Waking me up,
   Tickling my toes.

Reader Response

Let's Talk

How is your bedtime
like Biscuit's bedtime?
How is it different?

Let's Think

Who tells the story
about Pug?
Who tells the story
about Biscuit?
Which story do you
like better? Why?

Test Prep
Let's Write

Make a list of words that
tell about Biscuit.
Use your words to write
sentences about Biscuit.

Do a Puppet Show

Make puppets of Biscuit and the girl.
Use them to act out the story.

1

Draw faces on
paper bags.

2

Cut out ears, whiskers,
and hair.

3

Tape them on the
faces.

Now, act out the
story!

Language Arts

Special Names

People and pets have special names.
Special names begin with capital letters.

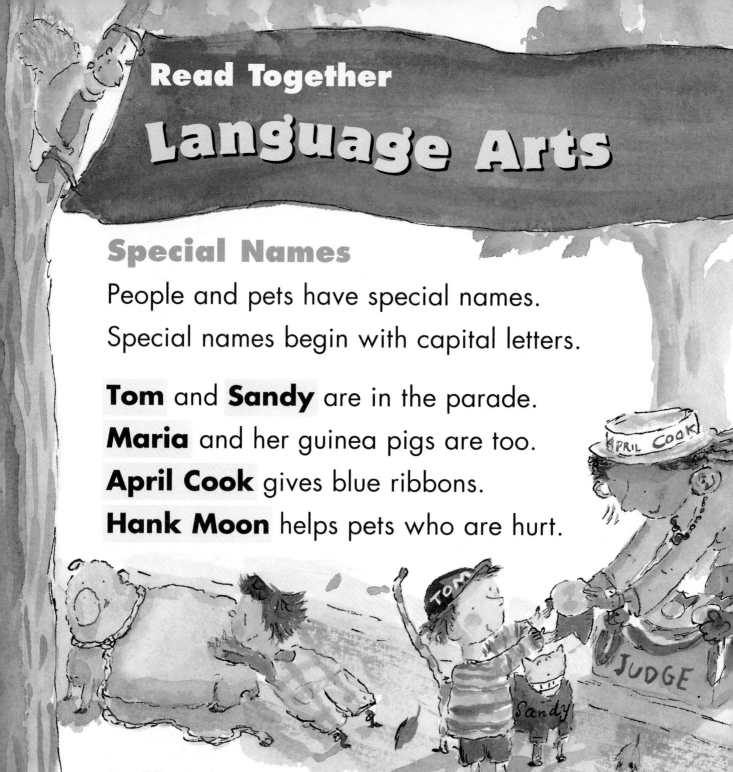

Tom and **Sandy** are in the parade.
Maria and her guinea pigs are too.
April Cook gives blue ribbons.
Hank Moon helps pets who are hurt.

Talk

Look at the pictures.
What special names do you see?
What capital letters do they
begin with?

Write

Write the sentences.

Circle the capital letter in each special name.

1. Benny hurt his foot.

2. Hank Moon helps Benny.

3. April Cook gives Sandy a ribbon.

Write your own sentences.

Use capital letters for special names.

Trucks

by Gail Saunders-Smith

Trucks carry logs.

Trucks haul garbage.

Trucks hold milk.

Trucks mix cement.

Trucks dump rocks.

Trucks plow snow.

Trucks tow cars.

Trucks bring mail.

Communities

by Gail Saunders-Smith

Police officers help
us stay safe.

Doctors help us
stay healthy.

Teachers help
us learn.

Coaches help
us play.

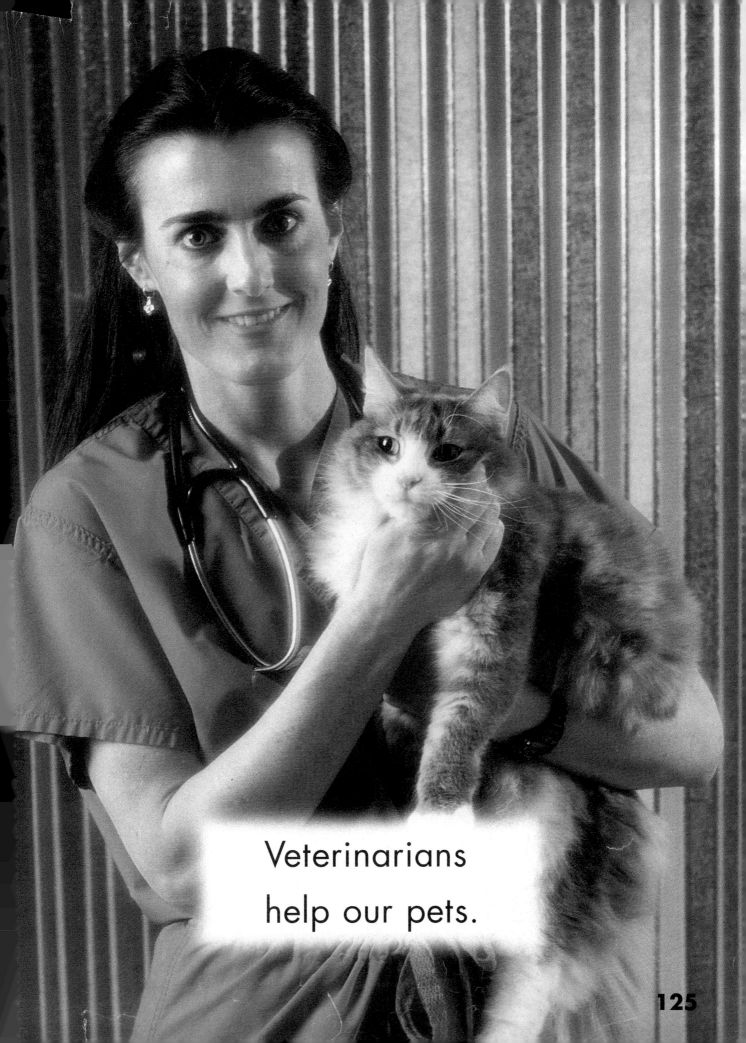

Veterinarians
help our pets.

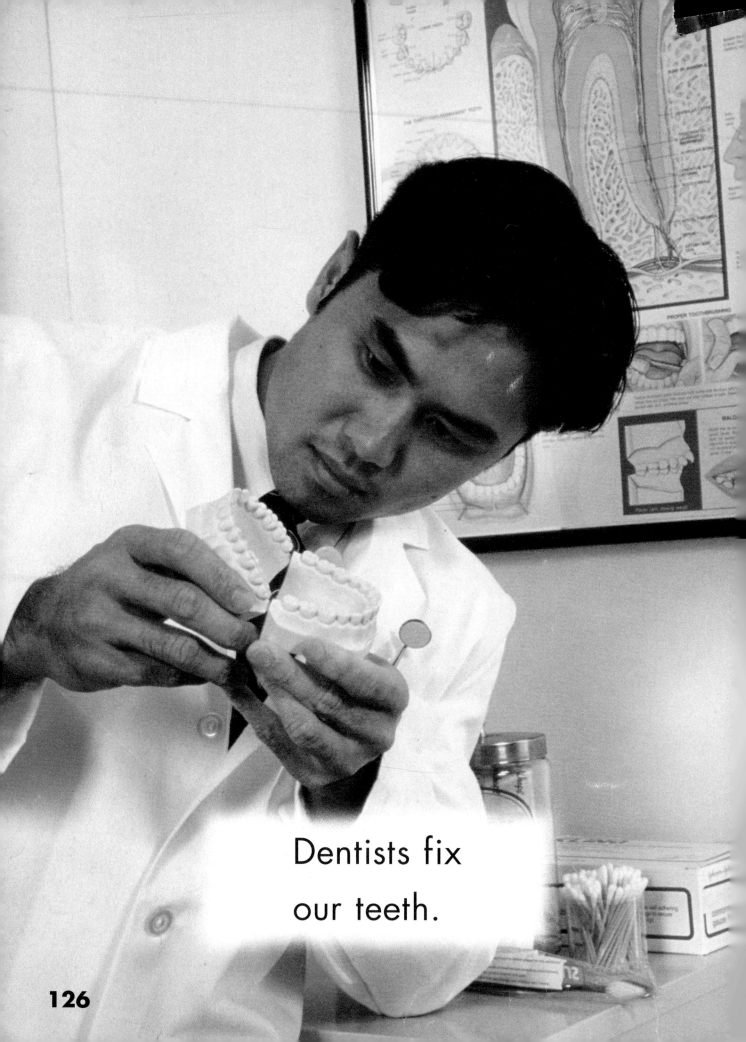

Dentists fix
our teeth.

Firefighters save
our homes.

Mail carriers
bring our mail.

Construction workers
build our roads.

Words to Know

coach—a person who trains a sports team

construction worker—a person who builds buildings or roads

dentist—a person who is trained to examine and fix teeth

doctor—a person who is trained to help people stay healthy

firefighter—a person who is trained to put out fires

mail carrier—a person who delivers or picks up mail

police officer—a person who is trained to make sure people obey the law

teacher—a person who is trained to show others how to do something

veterinarian—a person who is trained to treat sick and injured animals

About the Author

Gail Saunders-Smith
has written many nonfiction
books for young readers.
You know that she wrote
about trucks and communities.
She has also written about
nature and animals.

Reader Response

Let's Talk

You read about workers. Which workers have helped you the most? Tell how the workers helped.

Let's Think

What jobs did you read about? Why do you think they are important?

Test Prep
Let's Write

Who works in your school? Choose one person you would like to talk to. Write a question to ask about that person's job.

Interview at School

1. Talk to people who work in your school.

2. Ask them to visit your class.

3. Make name tags.

4. Ask questions.

403

Special Titles

A title can come before the
name of a person.
A title begins with a capital letter.
Some titles end with a **.** .

My mother is **Dr.** Meg Waters.

My teacher is **Mr.** Cal Smith.

- **Mr. Matt Dunn**
- **Judge Frank Lincoln**
- **Dr. Lila Horn**
- **Officer Kim Sing**
- **Ms. Sara Link**
- **Mayor Jan Zampa**
- **Mrs. Mary Novak**

Talk

What titles does the boy see?

What does the title tell you about the person?

What other titles do you know?

Write

Write the sentences.

Circle the special titles for people.

1. **Mr. Dunn is our neighbor.**
2. **Dr. Horn fixed my tooth.**
3. **Officer Sing is our crossing guard.**

Dr.

Coach

Nurse

Principal

Mrs.

Mr.

Write your own sentences.

Try to use special titles from the box.

Remember to add a **.** if you need to.

Circle the special titles.

Fox and Bear

by David McPhail

Fox ran to Bear's house.

136

Fox ran up.

Fox ran down.

Fox ran too fast.

Fox ran past the house.

Bear ran after Fox.

"Look," said Bear.

"Come back."

Fox came back.

He sat down for a chat.

"You can run fast," said Bear.

"Yes, I know," said Fox.

"I am glad you saw me!"
said Fox.

"I am glad too," said Bear.

Fox and Bear

Look at the Moon

by David McPhail

Fox and Bear sat.

"Look," said Bear.

"Look at the moon."

"It looks fat," said Fox.

"Yes, I know," said Bear.

"It does look fat."

Fox had a nap.

Bear sat and sat.

She looked at the moon.

The moon moved.

Bear gave Fox a tap.

Tap, tap.

"Look, Fox," said Bear.

"The moon is gone!"

Fox sat up.

"Where did it go?" asked Fox.

"Maybe it fell," said Bear.

Fox looked down.

There was the moon.

"I can get it out," said Fox.

"I can jump in!"

"Look," said Bear.

"The moon came back!"

"I got it out," said Fox.

"Yes, you did," said Bear.

Bear gave Fox a pat.

A big pat on the back.

Pat. Pat.

About the Author and Illustrator

David McPhail says that as a child he drew "anywhere, anytime, and on anything!" His love of drawing sometimes got him into trouble. He learned not to draw on walls!

Many of Mr. McPhail's books have animals in them. He really enjoys drawing bears.

Reader Response

Let's Talk

Fox says the moon
looks fat.
Does the moon always
look the same to you?
Why or why not?

Let's Think

Does Fox really get
the moon out of the
water? What
would you tell him?

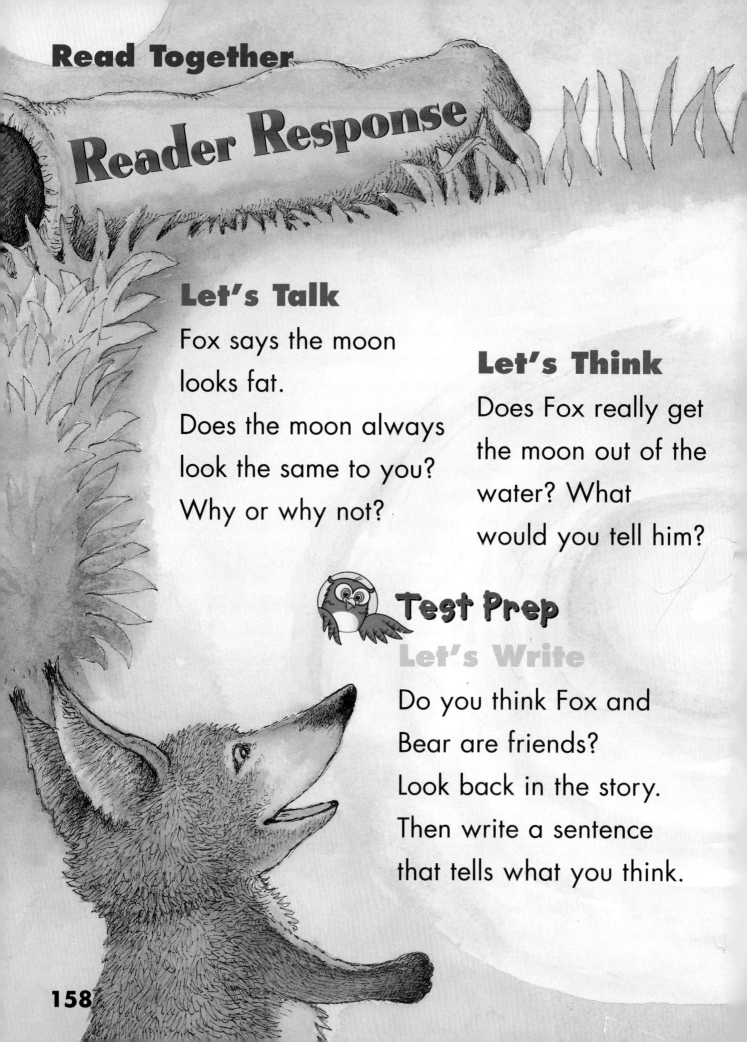

Test Prep
Let's Write

Do you think Fox and
Bear are friends?
Look back in the story.
Then write a sentence
that tells what you think.

Make a Class Book

Fox and Bear looked at
the moon together.
Think about other things
they might do together.
Work with others.
Make a book.

1. Draw pictures showing something
Fox and Bear might do together.

2. Punch holes at the edge of your
pictures.

3. Use yarn or ribbon to
tie the pages together.

Language Arts

Writing with Nouns

A noun can be in the
naming part of a sentence.
A noun can be in the
action part of a sentence.

naming part ↓	**action part** ↓
The **girl**	throws the **ball.**

Talk

Look at the pictures.
Then add nouns to the naming part
or action part of the sentences.

naming part	**action part**
___	ride the bikes.
The dog	runs next to a ___ .

Write

Write each sentence.

Circle the nouns.

1. Children play in the sand.

2. Mom pushes the swing.

3. The dog runs quickly.

Write your own sentences.

Use some nouns in the naming part.

Use some nouns in the action part.

I Can Read

by Judy Nayer

illustrated by Jennifer Beck Harris

I can read.

It's fun to do!

Please come with me.

I'll read to you!

I'll read the list
that's on this pad.

milk
nuts
six plums
ham
eggs
jam

I'll read the word
that's on my dad.

I'll read the words
there on the grass.

I'll walk and say
the words I pass.

Next come with me.

I know just where.

Yes! I see them!

More words are there!

The Den

lamps
rugs
beds
cribs

Hat Hut

hats
caps
wigs

Now I'll say
the words again.
Please read with me.
I'll bet you can!

Lilly Reads

by Laurie
Krasny Brown

illustrated by
Marc Brown

"Lilly," said Mrs. Woo,
"please read the next
page out loud.
Page six."

Lilly looked at page six.

She read,

"Long, long ago
in a far-off land,
there lived an elf
who was a bit of a . . ."

Lilly stopped.

"Very good, Lilly," said Mrs. Woo.
"Please go on."

Lilly looked at page six.
"I can't go on!" she said.
"I can't read the next word. It's too—"

"I can! I can!" Willy called out.

"But, Willy," said Mrs. Woo.

"It's Lilly's turn.

You can read this word, Lilly,"
she said.

"You can sound it out."

"It's too hard!" said Lilly.

Willy called out again,
"I can sound it out!
I can sound out this word."

"But, Willy, it's still Lilly's turn,"
said Mrs. Woo.
"Lilly, just try!"

So Lilly said the sounds out loud,

"P

   E."

"It's a short e, as in e*lf*," said Mrs. Woo.

"S

   T."

"Now say them again,"
said Mrs. Woo.

Lilly said them again.
"*P-e-s-t.*"
And again.
She said them faster.
And faster.

All of a sudden Lilly stopped
and looked at page six.
Then she read right out loud,
"Long, long ago
in a far-off land,
there lived an elf
who was a bit of a . . .
pest!"

"Yes!" said Mrs. Woo.
"Good work, Lilly!"

"And, Willy," said Lilly,
"that goes for you too.
You are a bit of a pest!"

Then Lilly read
and read
and read.

About the Author

Laurie Krasny Brown enjoys writing stories that young readers can read on their own.

Her husband, Marc Brown, drew the pictures for "Lilly Reads." He often does the drawings for her stories.

You can read more about Lilly and her brother, Rex. Ms. Brown has written several books about them.

Books Books Books

by Kay Winters

I LOVE TO READ!
Say those words.
Go those places.
See those sights.
Think those thoughts.
Meet those kids
who live in books,
waiting for me
to find them.

Reader Response

Let's Talk

Pretend that Lilly asks you to help her read. What would you tell her to do?

Let's Think

How did Willy make Lilly feel? Why do you think so?

Test Prep

Let's Write

Write the name of a book you think Lilly would like to read. Tell why you think she would like it.

Make a Bookmark

Lilly and Willy like to read.
Do you like to read too?
Make a Lilly or Willy
bookmark.

1. Draw the
head of Willy or Lilly.

2. Cut out your picture.
Don't forget to add hair.

3. Glue the head to the top
of a craft stick.

4. Use the bookmark to keep your
place in a favorite book.

Language Arts

Special Times

The names of days, months, and holidays begin with capital letters.

February

Sunday	Monday	Tuesday	Wednesday	Thursday	Friday	Saturday
1	2 Groundhog Day	3	4	5	6	7
8	9	10	11	12	13	14 Valentine's Day
15	16	17	18	19	20	21
22 Washington's Birthday	23	24	25	26	27	28

Talk

Look at the calendar.

What words begin with capital letters?

Find the names of the month and holidays.

Talk about other months and holidays.

Write

Write the sentences.
Draw a line under the names of the month, days, and holiday.

1. Thanksgiving is in November.

2. It comes on Thursday.

3. Grandma comes on Tuesday and stays until Sunday.

Use words from the box.
Write about a holiday.
What month is it in?
What day is it on?
Use capital letters.

Presidents' Day

April Fools' Day

Mother's Day

Father's Day

New Year's Day

The Big Mess

The Little Red Hen

help

now

said

so

who

Yes, We Want Some Too!

Cat Traps

for

good

some

too

want

My Buddy, Stan

Biscuit

jump

more

sleep

time

with

I Can Read

Lilly Reads

again

please

read

say

word

Trucks

Communities

bring

carry

hold

our

us

Fox and Bear

Fox and Bear

Look at the Moon

came

know

out

she

there

Understand the Question

Some test questions start with *Who*, *Why*, *Where*, or *When*. These words help you understand what the question is asking.

A test about *Communities* may have this question.

1. Who helps sick pets?

(A) coach

(B) veterinarian

(C) hospital

Read the question.

The important word is *Who*.

This word helps you understand the question.

Here is how one girl makes sure she understands the question.

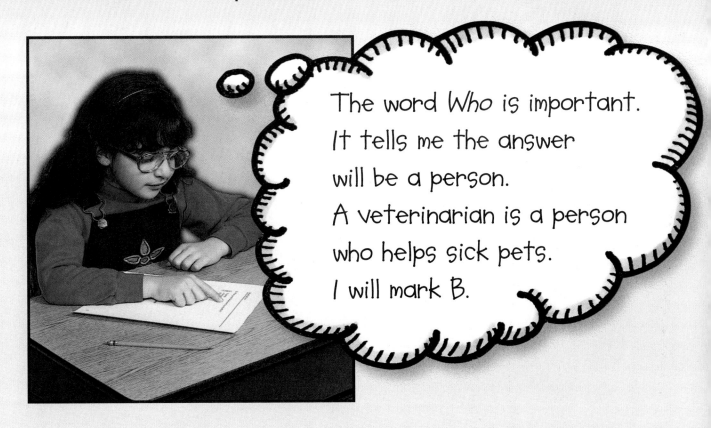

The word *Who* is important.
It tells me the answer
will be a person.
A veterinarian is a person
who helps sick pets.
I will mark B.

Try it!

Use what you have learned to understand
this test question about *Communities*.
Tell the important word in the question.

2. Who helps us learn in school?

(A) book

(B) doctor

(C) teacher

Things We Do

feed

carry

hold

sleep

read

190

191

Pictionary
More Things We Do

draw

cry

sing

kiss

listen

I can laugh!

hug

love

sneeze

wash

comb

brush

zip

button

tie

eat

drink

feed

heal

share

dance

Pictionary
More Things We Do

dive

fish

sail

kick

row

swim

watch

hop

jump

relax

punt

bend

swing

exercise

catch

throw

bounce

fly

skip

run

skate

ride

carry   surfboard

Pictionary
In the Kitchen

curtains

chair

table

window

wall

groceries

door

floor

bag

highchair

can

rug

mop

broom

toaster

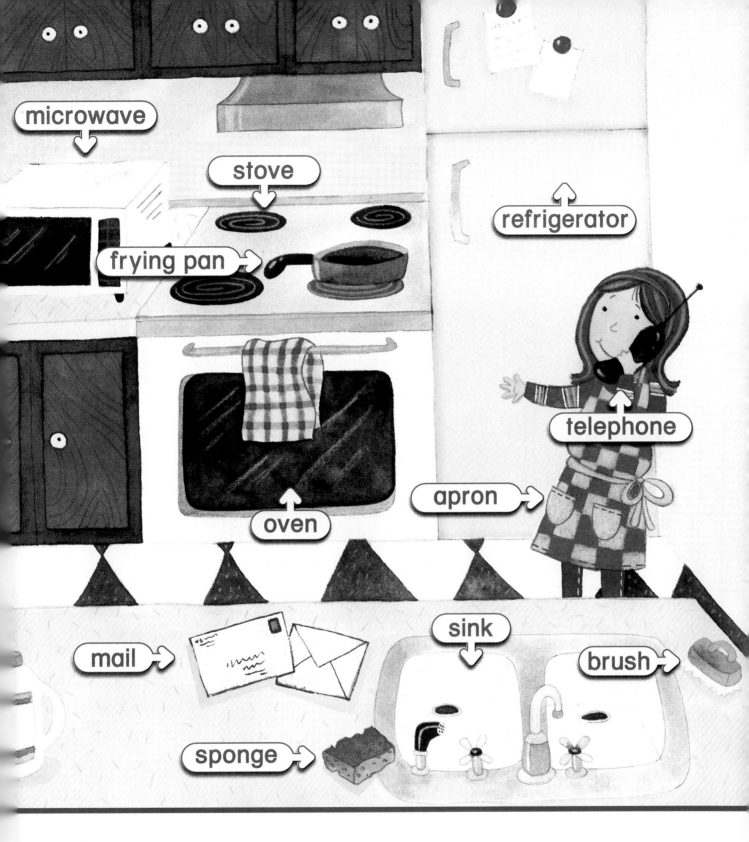

microwave

stove

frying pan

refrigerator

telephone

oven

apron

mail

sink

brush

sponge

clock

candle

newspaper

197

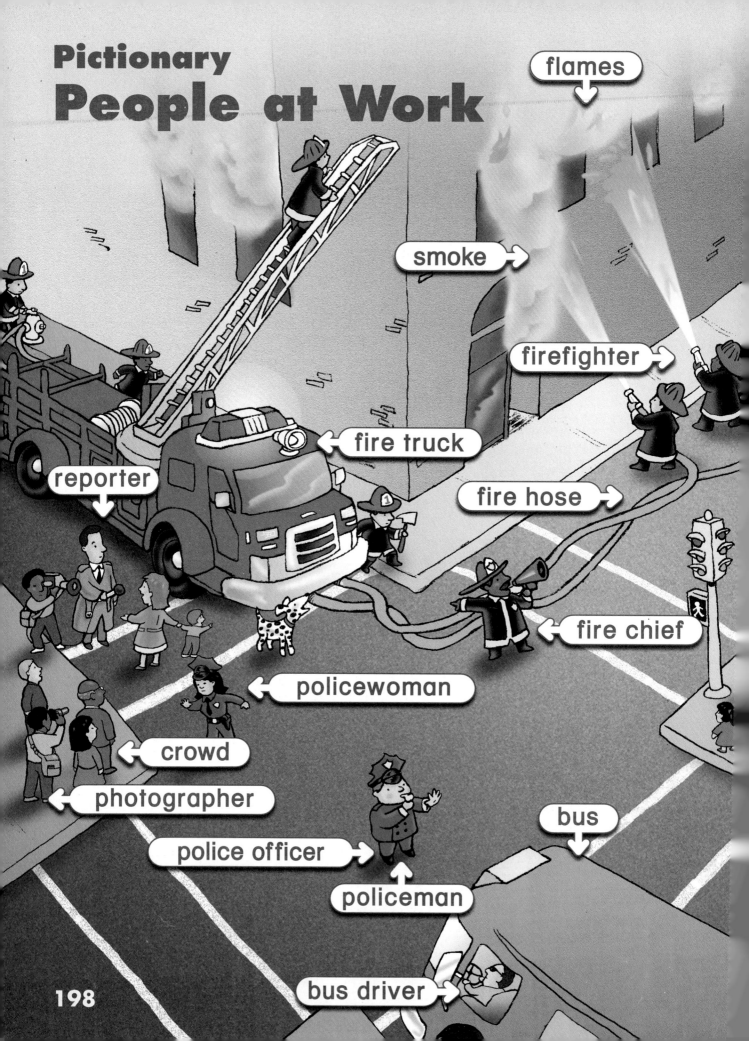

Pictionary
In the Classroom

clock

bulletin board

chalkboard

erase

easel

book

teacher

poster

cubbies

flag

bookcase

computer

blocks

backpack

chair

map

calendar

desk

lunchbox

backpack

notebook

clay

pencils

ruler

erasers

tape

chalk

glue

pencil sharpener

Pictionary
Months and Holidays

What is your favorite season? I love winter!

January

New Year

February

Valentine's Day

March

April

May

June

July

Fourth of July
Independence Day

August   September

October

November

Thanksgiving

December

Kwanzaa

Christmas

Hanukkah   **203**

Spelling Lists

The Big Mess
The Little Red Hen

1.	**red**	My hat is **red**.
2.	**bed**	Is it time for **bed**?
3.	**fed**	I **fed** the fish.
4.	**tell**	Can you **tell** me a story?
5.	**well**	Do you feel **well**?
6.	**mess**	This is a big **mess**.
7.	**fell**	The books **fell** off my desk.
8.	**yell**	Please do not **yell**.
9.	**said**	I **said** I do not know.
10.	**who**	**Who** will feed the hen?

Yes, We Want Some Too!
Cat Traps

1.	**met**	Mom **met** my new friend.
2.	**pet**	Do you have a **pet**?
3.	**let**	Will you **let** me play?
4.	**get**	What did you **get** for your birthday?
5.	**ten**	I have **ten** toes.
6.	**yes**	Mom said **yes**.
7.	**plan**	We will make a **plan**.
8.	**trap**	The cat set a **trap**.
9.	**want**	I **want** a new book.
10.	**good**	This pie is **good**.

My Buddy, Stan
Biscuit

1. **fun**   We had a **fun** day at the park.
2. **up**   The mouse ran **up** the clock.
3. **stuff**   Put your **stuff** here.
4. **run**   Don't **run** in the house.
5. **cup**   I had a **cup** of milk.
6. **puff**   I saw a **puff** of smoke.
7. **skip**   We like to hop and **skip**.
8. **swim**   Did you **swim** in the lake?
9. **jump**   Do not **jump** on the bed.
10. **more**   I want **more** pudding.

Trucks
Communities

1. **us**   The cake is for **us**.
2. **cut**   I **cut** the apple.
3. **rug**   We can sit on the **rug**.
4. **bus**   Mom took a **bus** to town.
5. **but**   I had it, **but** I lost it.
6. **hug**   I gave Dad a big **hug**.
7. **city**   The **city** has big buildings.
8. **giant**   A **giant** is very tall.
9. **our**   **Our** dog likes to play with the cat.
10. **bring**   Will you **bring** the cup to me?

Fox and Bear

Fox and Bear Look at the Moon

1. **and**   I ate bread **and** jam.
2. **fast**   Can you run **fast**?
3. **hand**   Hold out your **hand**.
4. **best**   My **best** work got a star.
5. **just**   I **just** ate a cookie.
6. **must**   I **must** be home by one o'clock.
7. **sent**   My aunt **sent** me a toy.
8. **next**   Who is **next** in line?
9. **out**   The boy went **out** the door.
10. **came** We **came** for a visit.

I Can Read

Lilly Reads

1. **clap**   Can you **clap** your hands?
2. **trip**   We took a **trip** to the zoo.
3. **drop**   Don't **drop** the cake.
4. **sled**   We rode a **sled** down the hill.
5. **spot**   I have a **spot** on my pants.
6. **drum**   Can you play a **drum**?
7. **can't**   I **can't** go to the show.
8. **it's**   **It's** a rainy day.
9. **read**   I can **read** a book.
10. **please** **Please** be my friend.

Tested
Word List

The Big Mess
The Little Red Hen

help
now
said
so
who

Yes, We Want
Some Too!
Cat Traps

for
good
some
too
want

My Buddy, Stan
Biscuit

jump
more
sleep
time
with

Trucks
Communities

bring
carry
hold
our
us

Fox and Bear
Fox and Bear
Look at the Moon

came
know
out
she
there

I Can Read
Lilly Reads

again
please
read
say
word

Acknowledgments

Text
Page 18: *The Little Red Hen* by Patricia and Fredrick McKissack, pp. 3–28 & 30. Copyright © 1985 by Regensteiner Publishing Enterprises, Inc. Reprinted by permission of Grolier Publishing Company.
Page 48: *Cat Traps* by Molly Coxe, pp. 4–32. Copyright © 1996 by Molly Coxe. Reprinted by permission of Random House, Inc.
Page 86: *Biscuit* by Alyssa Satin Capucilli, pictures by Pat Schories, pp. 6–26. Text copyright © 1996 by Alyssa Satin Capucilli. Illustrations copyright © 1996 by Pat Schories. Reprinted by permission of HarperCollins Publishers, Inc.
Page 107: "Puppy" Copyright © 1974, 1995 by Lee Bennett Hopkins. Appears in *Good Rhymes, Good Times,* published by HarperCollins Publishers. Reprinted by permission of Curtis Brown, Ltd.
Page 112: *Trucks* by Gail Saunders-Smith, pp. 5, 7, 9, 11, 13, 15, 17, 19, & 21–22. Copyright © 1998 by Pebble Books, an imprint of Capstone Press. Reprinted by permission of Capstone Press.
Page 120: *Communities* by Gail Saunders-Smith, pp. 5, 7, 9, 11, 13, 15, 17, 19, & 21–22. Copyright © 1998 by Pebble Books, an imprint of Capstone Press. Reprinted by permission of Capstone Press.
Pages 136, 144: © David McPhail.
Page 170: "Lilly Reads" from *Rex and Lilly Schooltime* by Laurie Krasny Brown, pictures by Marc Brown, pp. 23–32. Copyright © 1997 by Laurene Krasny Brown and Marc Brown. Reprinted by permission of Little, Brown and Company.
Page 181: "Books Books Books" from *Did You See What I Saw?* by Kay Winters, illustrated by Martha Weston. Text copyright © 1996 by Kay Winters. Illustrations copyright © 1996 by Martha Weston. Reprinted by permission of

Viking Penguin, a division of Penguin Putnam, Inc.
Selected text and images in this book are copyrighted © 2002.

Artists
Christine Davenier, 10–17
John Sandford, 4–5, 18–39, 186–187, 204–205
Rosario Valderrama, 40–47
Molly Coxe, 48–77
Shelly Hehenberger, 78–85
Pat Schories, 86–105
Laura Cornell, 108–111
Steven Mach, 132–135
David McPhail, 136–159
George Ulrich, 160–161
Jennifer Harris, 6–7, 162–169, 206
Marc Brown, 170–179
Martha Weston, 181
C. D. Hullinger, 182–185
Franklin Hammond, 188–189
Kathy McCord, 190–191
Anthony Lewis, 192–193
Keiko Motoyama, 194–195
Kelly Cottrell, 196–197
Michael Morris, 198
Paul Sharp, 199
David Austin Clar, 200–201
Clive Scruton, 202–203
Jennifer Fitchwell, 203

Photographs
Every effort has been made to secure permission and provide appropriate credit for photographic material. The publisher deeply regrets any omission and pledges to correct, in subsequent editions, errors called to its attention.
 Unless otherwise acknowledged, all photographs are the property of Scott Foresman, a division of Pearson Education. Page abbrevia-

tions are as follows: (t) top, (b) bottom, (l) left, (r) right, (ins) inset, (s) spot, (bk) background.
Page 107 Ron Kimball (B) Ron Kimball
Page 112 (C) Brian Atkinson/Valan Photos
Page 113 (T) H. H. Thomas/Unicorn Stock Photos
Page 114 (T) David R. Frazier/© David R. Frazier Photolibrary
Page 115 (TC) Jeff Greenberg/Unicorn Stock Photos
Page 116 (TC) J. A. Wilkinson/Valan Photos
Page 117 (T) Michael J. Johnson/Valan Photos
Page 118 (C) Florent Flipper/Unicorn Stock Photos
Page 119 (T) Aneal Vohra/Unicorn Stock Photos
Page 120 (TL) Arthur Tilley/FPG International LLC
Page 120 (TR) Tom Tracy/FPG International LLC
Page 120 (BL) James Blank/FPG International LLC
Page 120 (BR) Elizabeth Simpson/FPG International LLC
Page 121 (C) Michael Nelson/FPG International LLC
Page 122 (C) Mike Malyszko/FPG International LLC
Page 123 (C) Arthur Tilley/FPG International LLC
Page 124 (C) Andrew Farquhar/Valan Photos
Page 125 (C) Elizabeth Simpson/FPG International LLC
Page 126 (C) Tom McCarthy/Unicorn Stock Photos
Page 127 (C) Tom Tracy/FPG International LLC
Page 128 (C) James Blank/FPG International LLC
Page 129 (C) Bill Losh/FPG International LLC
Page 131 (TRC) Shock/Index Stock Imagery
Page 131 (CR) J. A. Wilkinson/Valan Photos
Page 131 (BL) Tony Joyce/Valan Photos

Pictionary
The contents of this pictionary have been adapted from *My Pictionary.* Copyright © 2000, Addison Wesley Educational Publishers, Inc., Glenview, Illinois.